she will never lose herself again

Jasmine Macias

i took my pain and turned it into art

welcome to my gallery

CONTENTS

for those hurting and those healing

introduction

i began writing this book after a breakup.
this was my way of expressing myself and releasing all the pain i was feeling inside.

originally, it was supposed to be filled with poems about brokenness only. because when i started writing that was all i felt, and i didn't believe those feelings would change. but as the months went by i started to heal. and so did my poetry.

together we went on a journey as i experienced every stage of a heart break. the good, the bad, and the ugly. when i was finished writing, i realized that right before my eyes was the entire healing process of a breakup. reading this book will feel as if you are diving deep inside the diary of a broken-hearted girl as she starts to find herself again.

it is somewhat nerve-racking publishing my thoughts on paper for the world to read. but the goal with this book is to empower anyone who needs the strength to pursue self-love. it is for the ones who lost themselves along the way of loving someone else. it is for you who is hurting. it is for you who is healing.

this is real life after heartbreak. healing is not linear. there will be good days and there will be bad days.

finding yourself does not happen overnight. as much as i know it hurts to hear, it is the truth. but i have learned through my own journey that it is important to not try and skip any phase you go through. embrace every moment you are in because they are all leading you into the best version of yourself. feel the pain. feel the regret. feel the anger. and grow from it.

this book is divided into five chapters and with every page you turn you can feel the growth of someone who was once lost begin to find herself again.

i like to believe this is a love story in some sort of a way.

you know how in typical love stories the girl and guy get married and live happily ever after in the end?

spoiler alert! not in this one. this girl saves herself. this girl put herself first. this girl doesn't end up with the guy.

she ends up with so much more.

this is a love story about falling back in love with myself.

pain is inevitable
you will hurt
you will cry

pain

the last love poem i wrote for you

you are magic
before you love was just a four-letter word
love songs were simply catchy tunes
and the moon was just the moon.

but after you,
love became the only word that mattered
every love song is about you
and what was once just a light in the night sky
is now something i compare you to in all my poetry.

you are the moon
a light in my darkness.
you move me like it moves the waves
and if the moon could feel
it would envy you
the way i not only compare you two
but the way i let you steal its shine.

my favorite thing about myself
is that i am loved by you

please do not go.

the first breakup poem i wrote for you

you are gone. i dream that we are on the beach. you tell me you are going to get us drinks and i wake up. i try to force myself to sleep so you can come back with our drinks but it is too late. i am crying on my bedroom floor with a broken phone that i threw across the room for waking me from being next to you.

i walk to the restroom and look in the mirror. i hear your voice whisper "you are beautiful." "no i am not," i say out loud. and your voice is gone. where did you go? it is silent.

i go downstairs to make breakfast and for a quick second, i can see you standing over the stove and cooking two eggs over easy just like we like them. when i run towards you, you are gone. the stove is off and i am no longer hungry.

i turn on the t.v and our favorite show is on. i quickly turn it off thinking how angry you would get if i watch it without you. but i then remember that we do not talk anymore. and i spend the next 30 minutes wondering if you have watched our shows without me.

i see you everywhere. and this is only the beginning. will i see you when i walk down the aisle towards someone else? will i see you when i am giving birth to my first child and he is holding my hand? will i wonder what our baby would have looked like?

i can't leave the house. it was supposed to be you. souls don't break up and you took yours from me.

i go lie down on my bed alone. i put two pillows next to me so it feels like you are there. i close my eyes and start to dream. and you are next to me. i say "oh my gosh, where have you been? i was so lonely." you say "i'm sorry. i was getting our drinks. i'm here now."

stage one: pain

it hurts to breathe
my heart is not broken
it is shattered

one moment you were the cause of my happiness
now you are the cause of the deepest pain
i have ever felt

our last night

i wondered how the hell you could fall asleep
while we were falling apart

i placed my head on your chest
and listened to your heart

all night i thought about us
the good, the bad
how the good wasn't enough

holding back tears
i listened to your heart again
tomorrow by this time
i will be alone in this bed

blur

i don't remember much after you left
everything is a blur for me these days

it feels as if i am living
inside the body of a stranger

i don't know
who i am without you

take me with you

you want to leave
and i don't blame you

i know i can't make you stay
you are desperate to get away

you want better days
but i want them too

as you walk out the door
i can't help but whisper
"please take me with you."

homeless

i should have known not to make a home out of you

but meeting you was like walking
through the door after a long vacation
home sweet home

i threw my bags on the floor and settled in

your laugh was my electricity
and your love was the gas
that started a fire in my soul

i spent years decorating the walls inside of you
leaving pieces of me in every hallway

my home was wherever you were

when you stopped loving me
my home began to feel different
the light i depended on burned out

and ashes were all that remained
where the fire once took place

when you left
my home went with you

now i am both homesick
and homeless

fearless

when i would get asked
what my biggest fear was
i blurted out something stupid
like heights or the mystery behind the ocean

but i conquered my fear of heights
when i jumped and fell for you

and i overcame my fear of water
when i loved you deeper than the ocean itself

i couldn't find the words to say
that the only thing that truly terrifies me
is losing you

i feared your absence
after having felt your company

the sound of silence
after hearing your laughter

the feeling of coldness
after being comforted by your warmth

now that you are gone
and i have faced my biggest fear
nothing scares me anymore
i am fearless

damaged goods

i knew it was too good to be true
for a person like you to fall in love with me

you were shiny and new
and i was damaged goods

maybe you liked the rush
or the adrenaline you'd get
walking around my broken pieces
trying not to get cut

you wanted to be the hero
who saved the girl that needed saving

when you realized
there was no reward
you left me all alone

now i am left
with more damage than before

never you

every time my phone rings
i hope it's you on the other line
but it never is

whenever a car passes by my house
i imagine it's you coming back to me
but it never is

it feels like i am waiting
for a moment that will never happen

because every time i hope it is
it's never you

movies

our first date was at the movies
years later in that same parking lot
we decided we were over

just like the arcade
that no longer exists
we are no longer together

our trailer was beautiful
but, misleading
and our ending
would have a crowd
demanding their refunds

as the end credits
appear on the screen

i must admit,
even though we didn't make the best movie
i still had my favorite scenes

miss me

do you miss me at all?
i don't think that you do
if you did you would call.

tell me what i can do
to make you miss me
the way that i miss you.

forever is 7 years, 4 months, and 3 weeks

i always said
looking at you felt like time travelling
i could see my future

you and me
in that house
we always said would be ours someday

right above the freeway
with the porch light always on

when you promised me forever
i could see our kids in the backseat
of the van we said we'd never buy

but we also said
we would never have kids
so we just laugh it off

unfortunately,
our forever only lasted 7 years, 4 months, and 3
weeks

there was no house on the hill
but we did rent a cozy apartment

there was no minivan
but i helped you buy your first car

and there were no kids
i will still be a mother someday
but you won't be their father

i know you meant it when you said forever
and i meant it too

but life had different plans for us
and our forever had a deadline

love me

of course
i wanted you to stay

i wanted to run after you
and beg you not to go

but i admired you
for having the courage to leave

you felt you deserved better
and better was not me

i cannot hate you
for loving yourself

i can only wish
to someday love me
the way that you, love you

he loves me not

a dozen roses later
too many petals to count on the floor
i'm looking for a sign from the universe
a simple glimpse of hope
that you still love me
the way you once did
my heart never comprehended
what my head already knows

every time my phone rings
i answer in an apologetic voice
just in case it's you
and when there's a knock on the door
i fix my hair up the way you used to like it
just in case you're on the other side

but those scenarios are impossible
because we're not who we used to be

you took a piece of my heart with you
and i miss it

i keep telling myself
it's okay to feel emptiness
in the place you once filled

but for now
i'll keep buying roses
and with every petal i detach

i'll whisper to myself
he loves me not
he loves me not
until my heart believes it

teach me

you make moving on look easy
teach me

because here i am
sitting in my room
wondering how the hell you're at a bar

i spent my night crying in bed
you spent yours out with friends

i wonder if you're hurting too
or if i'm just easy to forget

bed rest

the pillowcases where i lay my head to rest
know the taste of all the tears i've cried for you

i cannot recuperate the strength
to get myself off of this bed

9:20 p.m.

it's nine twenty p.m.
and our song is playing on the radio

i sing every lyric at the top of my lungs
hoping if I yell loud enough
my voice will reach you

i close my eyes and imagine you're with me
and for a second i feel a wave of happiness

but at nine twenty-four
the song came to an end

just like we did

dreams

the nights we slept on the same bed
i would have nightmares
about losing you

and it was the most beautiful feeling
waking up with you by my side

now that you are gone
i dream of you coming back to me

and it is the most heartbreaking feeling
waking up to an empty bed

friends

how dare you
ask if we could still be friends?

i know what it's like
to feel your touch
your kisses

i've seen you naked
in the shower
and in bed

i can't be just friends with someone
i was willing to follow straight into hell
if it meant we could be together

texts i almost sent last night

hi
delete

how have you been?
delete

i'm sorry for everything
delete

hey
your favorite song just played on the radio
and i thought of you
delete

remember the night
we danced in my backyard
and you promised you'd love me forever?
delete

i miss you...
please tell me you miss me too
delete

message to my heart

i finally accept that
we were no good for each other
and walking away
was what i had to do

but my heart doesn't understand
because it aches for you
from the moment i wake up
till the second i fall asleep again

i spend my days crying on the bathroom floor
trying to figure out how to send a message
from my head to my heart
so the pain will finally stop

i put both hands on my chest
to feel my heartbeat

i say,
"dear heart
i know you once beat for him
but he is gone now and it was for the best."

but the pain continues
and i can feel the message my heart is sending back
"i miss him..."

no regrets?
i have many

regret

stage two: regret

i cannot live my life with no regrets
i should've said i love you more often
i should've hugged you tighter
i should've kissed you longer

countdown

after you left,
every moment i took for granted
rushed into my mind

the nights you begged me to go to bed with you
but i stayed up watching television
because I wasn't tired yet

the days i sent you to the store alone
when all you wanted was
my company on your passenger seat

and all those countless hours i spent on my phone
while you were sitting right across from me

i should have gone to bed with you

i should have went with you to every location

i should have put my phone down
and talked to you instead

if i had known
somewhere there was a clock
counting down the time we had left together

i would have made the best out of every second

haunted

i'm being haunted
by the thoughts of what could've been

i hear the echoes of laughter
from the children we didn't have

cold shivers fill my body
as i imagine you and i together at 40

we were so close
i can see and feel a future we almost made

i know we ended
but the haunting of us is just beginning

come back

okay, shows over
the crowd applauses
the curtains have closed
come back.

yes, i found self-love again
and i promise i have learned my lesson
come...back.

people keep telling me
if it's meant to be
we will be someday
but someday needs to be today
come...... back.

you aren't coming back
are you?

alternate universe

you once told me you believed in many universes
an infinite number of different versions of us

you'd say in one world we have our dream job
and in the other we have our dream house

i laughed at how cruel that theory was
because it doesn't give us everything
we want in one life

but now that we are over
i know in this universe
i don't get you

i like to believe that in another life
it's a sunny tuesday
and we are having a picnic by the water
eating our favorite foods
and i am still yours

that is the universe
i would love to be in

start over

can we start over?
i promise it will be different

i know everything you hated about me
so i will become everything you love

i'll ignore the little things
instead of making a big fight

there are so many things
we did not get to do
we needed more time

maybe i can make you fall in love again
please give us a chance to start over

memorize

as the months pass
i am starting to forget you

my nose can no longer
remember your scent

my lips can no longer
remember how it feels to kiss yours

what does your laugh sound like again?
i need to remember
because it was the reason i told so many jokes

i am terrified that one day
i will forget you completely

and i don't want to live in a world
where my mind doesn't recall

all the little details
i spent years memorizing about you

my fault

you met me when i was thinner
but over the years i put on some weight
i'm sorry if my body no longer attracted you

when you complimented my beauty
i would accuse you of lying
i'm sorry i was never confident
and my insecurities took over

you always wanted someone
to match your energy
but i was drained from my past
i'm sorry i was always tired

i could spend lifetimes apologizing
so i'll leave it at this

we did not end up together
and that is my fault

lost

we went our separate ways
but i like to believe

that maybe we were meant to get lost
so we could find ourselves

and when it's all done
maybe we can find each other again

moon

when we first met
i talked to the moon about you

months later
we kissed under the stars
and you told me
if i ever missed you
to look up at the sky

and no matter how far
remember that we are always under the same moon

when we fell apart
i cried to the moon about you

now i am sitting here
thinking of you
staring at the moon
and wondering
are you looking up too?

prince charming

when i was a little girl
i believed one day
my prince charming would show up at my doorstep
ready to save me

we would get married
and live happily ever after.

but prince charming didn't show up
on a horse with my slipper
he showed up in cargo shorts
and his favorite black t-shirt.

and he couldn't save me

but he tried

he handed me the glass slipper
and it shattered as i threw it across the room

he kissed my lips
and tried to wake me from my nightmares
but they followed me in daylight

he begged me not to consume the poisonous apple
but i ate it till every part of me was rotten

i was his beauty and his beast
but the beast in me took over

i held him captive
and he lost himself in my castle

the day he finally understood
that this princess could not be saved
he escaped

maybe i should have saved myself
instead of waiting for prince charming

now my fairytale has no happy ending

i love you
i hate you
fuck you

anger

stage three: anger

when i hear your name
i am instantly filled with anger

i hate myself for loving you too much
i hate you for not loving me enough

therapy

i walked into therapy
in hopes it would change me
so i can be a better me for you

when my therapist implied
you were no good for me
i defended your name every time

but she untangled the knots in my mind
and cleared the fog that you once put there

now i see you differently
now i see the truth

you were no good for me
in fact, you were no good at all

now i hate you

i thought hating you
would make losing you easier

when i loved you
all i wanted to know
was that you were okay

all my thoughts were wasted on you
and everything reminded me of you

so, i wished i could hate you
thinking it would take the pain away

now that i hate you
all i want to know
is that you are not okay

all my thoughts are still wasted on you
but this time it's like an
infection that keeps spreading

i don't know what i crave more
you, finally out of my head
or revenge

power

i cannot believe
there was a moment you told me
without you i would die

i owe myself an apology
for ever giving a man the impression
he had that much power

you are not worth the end of my life

i wish i never met you

although there were good times
no amount of good makes up for the bad ones

and the happiness you made me feel
will never be worth the sadness you instilled in me

it is said that it's better to have loved and lost
than to have never loved at all

but your love created a monster in me
that i will spend forever trying to tame

so, that phrase means nothing to me
meeting you will always be my biggest regret

the worst

i don't wish you the worst
but i don't wish you the best

i hope you find someone you love
but that someone loves you less

i hope you get a job with great pay
but get stuck with a manager you hate

i hope you get approved for the apartment
but then they raise the rent

i don't hate you enough to wish the worst
but i don't love you enough to wish the best

toxic

when you could no longer control me
you tried to control the way others view me

you spit on my name
and spread lies like venom

thank you for showing me your true colors
it made getting over you so much easier

least compatible

i ignored every sign
even your own fucking sign

i should've known stars never lie
and stayed away from geminis

growth

you were a seed when i met you
but i saw the potential flower
you could one day bloom into

everyone told me you were just a weed

despite it all
i watered you every day
in hopes you would grow

i faced you towards the sun
and gave you all my warmth
so you'd survive

but in the end
it wasn't enough

because you were just a weed
prepared to stop my growth
and steal my sunlight

you are no longer welcome in my garden

you'll think of me

you try to fill the gaps
of loneliness with distractions

you turn the radio up on drives home
hoping the sound can drown out your own thoughts

you chug the bottle of vodka
because passing out on the floor means
you won't have to go home to a bed that i am not in

but you'll still think of me

when the music stops playing
in between the second of silence
before the next song starts
you'll think of me

about how my laughter
would have filled the silence
and how much you miss me on the passenger seat

you will think of me on the walk
from your house to your car

you will think of me when you close
your eyes and start to drift off to sleep

those in-between moments
will always be filled with thoughts of me

dirty secret

i could tell them
the promises you made
and never kept

i could tell them
how you changed me
in the worst ways

i could tell them
what you said
that turned me into a monster

i could tell them
all about your provoking
that caused my retaliation

but i'll keep your dirty secrets
and let them call me crazy
we both know that's how you made me

drunk text

it's 3am and you're intoxicated
texting me about my toxic traits you hated

blaming me as always for us falling apart
saying i'm the reason you have a broken heart

i won't respond to your text message
i know you just want a reaction

you see me doing better without you
and you cannot stand it

tomorrow when you're sober
and this anger passes over
you will regret every word you sent

go cure your hangover
i just blocked your number
i never want a drunk text from you again

so now you're back

the word has reached you
or you did some research
and you didn't like what you heard

suddenly your world came crumbling down
and you felt the pain that i had felt for months
but what you felt was worse

you saw that i moved on
and not to someone else
to myself

which you assumed would hurt less
but now you're realizing
that maybe you could take me from another man
but you cannot compete with a woman
filled with self-love

so, now you're back
thinking maybe a text from you will get a response
or that the door will open for you
if you show up outside my house

you're doing everything i thought i wanted
but now it's you that i don't want

bullet

everything about you was bad for me

you were a bullet, i dodged it
i guess it wasn't my time to go yet

living without you

i thought i couldn't live without you
but now i realize i was dying with you

because being with someone
who does not see your worth is draining

it was a full-time job trying to show you
all the reasons why i deserved to be loved
and i was exhausted

i started to believe maybe you were right
when you told me i was hard to love

i thought giving up on us
would kill me

but the day i left
i felt more alive than i ever did by your side

irony

i sent you a friend request and we met online
now i have you blocked on every social media

we once said we would never lose contact
now i just deleted your number off my contacts

someone new

i met someone new
and he is everything that you are not

when i'm around him i feel peace
being around you felt like a storm

he looks at me with eyes full of love
you looked at me with a heart filled with hate

i like that he brings out the best in me
you always brought out the worst

i know i shouldn't compare the two of you
but i need to look for you in every man i meet

so if i get a glimpse of similarities
i can run the other way

i spent so much of my time
angry that you did not show me what love was

but now i am thankful
that you showed me exactly what love was not

his lips tasted like him

i feared the day i would kiss someone new
i was not ready to feel his lips
but taste yours

i didn't want to close my eyes
and think of you
only to open them
and see someone else

but it was inevitable
and i knew the day would come
where i had to face this fear
and it did

his lips were smaller than yours
but still beautiful

he was much taller
which made it hard to picture you
he leaned in and kissed me
and his lips tasted like, well him.

so, i wrapped my arms around his neck
and kissed him back
it felt like someone new
and i loved that

i guess you didn't have as much of an impact
as i imagined

lesson learned

you are the story i will tell my daughter
when she experiences her first heartbreak

i will tell her about my greatest lesson ever learned
the time i loved someone else more than myself

i will tell her how loud your silence was
and how lonely your presence made me feel

i will tell her of all the things you ruined
including myself

and how you can't change a person
who does not want to be changed

after she hears all the pain i endured
she will know two things

one, how cruel a human can be
and two, never love someone else
more than you love yourself

wasn't

he was nice
until he no longer wasn't

and it was love
until he no longer felt it

believe

you want to believe
he will change
but he never will

now you are suffering
wondering why you are not enough
to make a man want to be better

please understand
it has nothing to do with you

it is time for you to go
and let him experience his greatest loss

recovery

now that i've spent some time away from you
the fog that once distorted my vision is gone
and i can see everything much clearer

i romanticized you in every way
i wanted to be loved like the princesses
in all my favorite childhood movies
so i created a fairytale that only existed in my head

i was young
and you were the first boy to show interest in me
so i ignored every red flag as if i could see no color

i only cared that you wiped away my tears
completely disregarding that you
were the reason they formed

i traced your face with my fingers
making patterns with your freckles
and all i could think about
was how can someone so perfect choose me?

you were my addiction
i would follow you across the world if needed

when you changed for the worst
every part of my being still craved you
and even though you started to break me
you were still the only one that could fix me

deep down i knew you were bad for me

but i made excuses
because at least it wasn't drugs
that was rotting my insides
it was you

now that i have finally gotten away
i still feel the need to go back at times

but just like any other addiction
it is time for me to recover from
all the damage that you created

sunrise

when the sun is finished setting
and the moon makes an appearance
you will think of me

regardless of what phase it's in
you will look up at the sky
and remember how i once was your light
in times of darkness

your mind will spiral from that thought
and force you to remember
how significant the moon was to me

the way i always told you i loved you to it and back
and how i never missed a chance
to take a picture when it was full

you will learn to love the sunrise
and you will despise the sunsets

before you look for me

if ever my absence
has you yearning for my presence
think again

i have changed in every possible way
you would not recognize me

you miss someone who no longer exists
and when you come to that realization

you will mourn just as i did
when i killed that version of myself

i cannot give you the closure you seek

so, before you come look for me
think again
and don't.

allow me to reintroduce myself

when you left
i left with you

and i don't mean that romantically
as if you took a piece of me in your heart
you took all of me.

and i don't mean that in a painful way
as if there was nothing left inside

but you took the me that i was with you

the girl who put her self-worth in your hands
and loved you more than she loved herself

i am not the same person
you left standing in our driveway

i have changed in ways
you would not believe are possible

so, if you ever see me
do not go up to me and greet me
you do not know who i am anymore

allow me to reintroduce myself

to the girl after me

i could tell you about his best qualities
the reasons why it took longer to leave

but i prefer to warn you
about his not so best ones instead

the reasons i finally left
all the little things you won't see coming

like his way of sneaking in insults
to make you feel less than
but don't believe them
he's just insecure

he will ask for your opinions on every decision
before he makes it
do not mistake it as being valid
he just needs someone to blame
in case things go wrong

every moment will feel like walking on glass
because he tends to throw your past at your face
no matter how hard you try to change

and when you suspect he's lying, he probably is
he was never good at keeping secrets

i am not trying to scare you off
you will see him at his best, he will take care of that
but you need to be warned about his worst

betrayal

after everything i did for you
you betrayed me in the worst ways

there was a time you protected me from evil people
but now you are the person i need protection from

all my pain i cried to you about
was now being caused by you

i am now traumatized at the thought
that someone who once made you feel alive
can be the same person who makes you want to die

i set myself free

you made me feel trapped
like a tree with roots so deep
it could never leave

you made me feel caged
and i was too busy
making sure you learned how to fly
i didn't notice you cutting my wings

pushing you forward
meant i always had to stand behind you

somewhere deep down
i knew i was capable of more than you said i was

so, i set myself free
from the chains
you had on me

from the cage
you kept me in

now that i have felt the wind against my wings
i will never return

abuse

i have found the one thing
worse than being abused

it is
having to watch
as the audience
applauds your abuser

not sorry

i am not sorry for choosing myself
i only regret not choosing myself sooner

last poem i wrote about you

today my heart said no
no i won't feel an ache when i hear his name
no i won't crave a man who caused me pain

today my mind said no
no i do not want to think about him anymore
no i will not be reminded of him every time
i step out the door

today when i picked up the pen, my hand said no
no i refuse to write about him
it is time to write about something different

i cannot create art with no inspiration
and the thought of us
no longer makes me feel passion

so, this is my last poem for you
you will die on this page

and still
you are not worthy
of me mentioning your name

i loved
i lost
i let go

acceptance

stage four: acceptance

sometimes your first love
is not meant to be your last

maybe this heartbreak was needed
to guide you in the arms
of your true first love,
yourself.

abandoned home

i think the best part about losing you
is that now i have found me

i spent every moment giving you all my love
i didn't realize i left none for myself

when you left,
it felt like i walked through the doors
of an abandoned home

i could feel the loneliness
of a place that once had company
i could hear the echo of a laughter
that once filled those halls

i started to redecorate the parts of my soul
that had been left unfinished
while i was too busy making a home out of you

i planted flowers in my heart
and watered them with care
i tore down every web
and memory of you that consumed my mind

and before i knew it
the remodeling was finished
move in ready

i will never leave this home unattended again

rebuild

getting lost in your chaos
made me want to find my peace

your hatred towards me
led me to crave love for myself

if what i needed
was to be destroyed by you

so that i could rebuild myself
into the person i am today

then it was worth it

stay away

before you left
you said we were bad people

but the difference between us
is i let you go
and hoped you would grow

even though it hurt
i kept my distance
to let you find happiness without me

but you saw me grow
and did not like it

when you realized i was happy without you
you brought chaos back into my life
and tried to bring me down with you

you were right
we were both bad people

but i changed
and you are the same

goodbye letter

we sat in the room 5 feet apart from each other
tears filled both our eyes as we wrote our goodbye
letter

we wrote about how much love we both had
but we had to split up because we both became sad

i don't remember what else the letters read
but here's what i should have written instead

"i know that right now we are both lovers
but in 2-3 months, we will become strangers
and all the good things you say you wish for me,
you'll take it all back when you start to get angry

i can't tell you that we'll still be friends
the truth is our friendship has also come to an end

i'll block your phone number
and you'll block me online

at first it will hurt
but we'll both heal in time

so, thank you for all the good times that we had
i hope someday you forgive me
like i forgive you for the bad."

the day you left, i found myself

the day you left, i found myself
sitting on the bathroom floor with puffy red eyes
holding on to your sweater to take in
the scent you left behind

i looked in the mirror and said, *"are you okay?"*
to my surprise, she replied
"where have you been?
you lived for him so i have died.
he was our everything and now that he's gone
we don't have anything."

the week after you left, i found myself
crying in the shower reminiscing about us
but at least i finally got out of bed, right?

the month after you left, i found myself
sitting at the kitchen table ready to eat
because my appetite came back

i found myself when i started to laugh again
and all the moments i picked myself up

i love who i found

delete

today i decided to quit avoiding our photos
as i scrolled through our albums
i examined every picture

trying to find clues
that would lead me to
the moment things went wrong

but photographs are not real
i realized that when i came across
the photo you took of me after our big fight

you would never know
that was the face of a girl
who had just been told she was not enough

i will not find answers hidden in our pictures
you are gone and i must accept that
now every photo of us is deleted

myself first

this is the part of my story where i put myself first
so i am leaving you

as hard as it will be
it must be done

you do not give anymore
all you do is take
and i am running out of what i have left to give

what is left
belongs to me

i need to let you go
before you leave me empty

the good in this goodbye
is finally ridding myself of you

i love myself more

dear lover,

you must understand that i will love you
but i will love myself more

what this means is

you will not be my other half
because i alone am whole

i will not do anything for you
i have lines that i will not cross

i will not be here no matter what
you have lines that you cannot cross

because if you do
i will leave as quickly as i arrived.

i put myself second before
and i will never do that again

so, if you want to make this work
understand that i will always love myself more

heal

when you heal
do not forget what broke you

and whatever or whoever that was
never go back

self-worth

i am worth more
than what i allowed myself to go through

i deserve to heal and find my peace
so that i never let that happen again

reflection

when i found myself
staring at my reflection
wiping away my own tears
taking in a deep breath
and letting it out

i realized
how strong i really am

i watched
as i put myself back together
and what a beautiful thing that was to see

same, but different

i saw you for the first time in months today
you looked the same, but different

your brown eyes were still droopy
but the bags under revealed
you hadn't been sleeping

i could tell by your arms
that you have been going to the gym
but your belly showed
that you have also been drinking

you looked lost and broken
i would notice that look anywhere
it was me the month after we broke up

but most importantly
the biggest difference was
i didn't love you anymore

i looked you in your eyes and felt free
knowing those eyes no longer held a piece of me

i needed to see you
to show myself that i was over you
and i am

you told me you were broken
but it is not my job to fix you anymore

love story

once upon a time
we were my favorite love story
but every story has an ending

there will be no sequel to our book
it ends here.

deserve better

we were two people who deserved the best
but with each other we settled for less

you were less for me
and i was less for you

no matter how hard we tried
to be better for one another
it could never work

because we deserved the best
and my best was someone else

new lover

i never thought
i would feel this way again

i believed last time
was the last time
i would let someone else in

all i've ever known
was love to be a storm

but you have shown me
that it can be peaceful

i look forward to entering
a healthy relationship with you

still

now that the hate has left my heart
and i have no ill feelings towards you

i suppose i still wish you the best

i hope you do everything you said you would
and reach every goal you set for yourself

closure

this is for you
seeking my closure
i know you have questions
you would love for me to answer

so i will tell you this
and when you finish reading
please close the chapter of us

i loved you then
it wasn't an act
the feelings were real

unfortunately,
that was the only way i knew how to love
so i apologize if it was not enough

but our love faded
and the more we tore each other down
the more i loved you less and less

i know i hurt you
you hurt me too
and yes,
if i could go back i would do things differently

i don't know why
we were meant to meet but not be

maybe we will get answers someday
but don't count on me to give them to you

and if ever you wonder
if i regret you
the answer is no

i do not regret meeting you
i do not regret loving you

but i also do not regret losing you
because that was the beginning of freedom
for the both of us

it doesn't happen overnight
but before you know it
you stop crying in the shower
and you start to sing again

healing

stage five: healing

the greatest feeling you will ever experience
is the healing that comes after the hurt

you've hit rock bottom
and watched as you got back up

now that you understand
you have the power to heal yourself

absolutely nothing can break you anymore

self-care

right now
a face mask is not what you need
you need to delete the photos of him off your phone

a shopping spree will not help
you need to stop checking his social media

sometimes the best form of self-care
is letting go

so, let go
you will not know the feeling of freedom
until you release what you are holding on to

the old me

she always hid behind large sweaters and sunglasses
thinking maybe if she hides herself
she'll be judged less

there were two things she never knew
self-love and her worth

she couldn't accept compliments
because her insecurities convinced her
that they were lies

and her free time was spent trying to fix men
hoping if she did a good enough job
they would love her the way she deserved

but that was the old me
i will never be her again

when you heal

you will feel confused at first
you've spent so long with that weight on your heart
you almost start to miss the heaviness
that used to fill its place

your mind will start to wonder, why now?
why did you not leave sooner?
and you will start to feel angry at yourself
for taking this long

different emotions will take over
where the brokenness once was

and you will feel both happiness and sadness
at the same time

it will be the most bittersweet feeling

but when you heal,
and all the broken pieces are put back together
you will understand exactly why it took this long

and you won't pay mind to what broke you
you will only focus on the strength
that came from it

first

love yourself first
the rest of the world can wait

searching

i searched
for a love that was pure

a love that would make me feel whole
and a place to call home
both comfortable and safe

a love i could trust would never die out

i searched for this love in every person i met
and in return, i broke my own heart
waiting for a love that no one was offering

but still i craved it day and night
thinking i would travel the world just to find it

not knowing,
i didn't need to take even the smallest step
because the love i desired was self-love

find yourself

you cannot find yourself
until you have lost yourself

so now that you are missing
search for every part of you

go as far as you must
do whatever it takes

and do not stop until every piece of you is found

california

i finally made it to california

i did not understand why it took this long
until i stepped foot in los angeles

i was never meant to go on this trip
with someone else
this was a moment i had to take in all by myself

i finally made it to venice beach
i gave my undivided attention to the waves
as they hit the shore
and soaked in all the comfort from the ocean breeze

i finally made it to hollywood boulevard
and i didn't just walk across the stars
i danced on them
yelling at the top of my lungs
"my name will be here someday!"

i found a part of myself in california

to my younger self

you'll make it far
i know this because i'm taking you there

what now?

the second he walks out the door
you ask yourself
what now?

i will tell you
now you live
now you make new friends
or reconnect with old ones

now you do all the things
you kept putting off
while you were invested in him

and with every bone inside your body
start to pick yourself back up

stand in front of the mirror
and tell yourself that you will be okay
because you will

but whatever you do
please do not shrink

use this time to grow

to my mother

God bless the person
who holds you when you are broken.
for me, that was you.

sometimes i wonder if my heartbreak
broke you more than it broke me.

it must have been painful
to watch your daughter in pain.

thank you for taking care of me
when i didn't have the strength to care for myself.

you reminded me every day
that i am worthy and deserve happiness.

today i am the best version of myself
and i owe so much of that to you.

best friend

the universe was saving you
for the worst moment of my life

only you could help bring me up
from the dirt i was left in

thank you for reminding me
to look up at the moon again

a letter to the girl that is holding on

leave
i know you feel like your world will come to an end
but darling, it will just begin

leave
you can live without him
you can be on your own

he is an insignificant man
he is not your home

leave
i beg you to go
because you deserve so much more

more than this unhappy life
that you are settling for

for those who move on to someone else

are you ready?
or are you trying to fill a void?
have you found self-love?
have you healed?

it is okay to be alone
whatever you have heard before
it's all lies
loneliness is not the worst thing in the world
but you know what's not okay?

moving on when you are not ready
you will hurt someone new for avoiding healing

i know you don't care
all you want is to move forward

but sometimes

the best upgrade
the best person to move on to
is yourself.

for those who move on to themselves

you are ready
the void you feel right now will be filled
you will find self-love
you will heal

it is okay to be alone
whatever you have heard before
it's all lies
loneliness is not the worst thing in the world
and in time
you will come to realize just that

find yourself again
love yourself

the best upgrade
the best person to move on to
was always you

never be the same

the truth is
you will never be who you were
before the heartbreak
it is better you know this now

so instead of trying to be the old you
embrace this new person

don't run from growth
run towards it

the new you is a bad ass
stronger than ever before
fall in love with her

to the heartbroken

do not stop yourself from crying over him
imagine your body is filled with a bucket of tears
and it is your job to empty it
afterwards, you will hurt a little less

gather every photograph and object
that reminds you of him
and put it in a box out of your sight
i know you still have hope
that he will be back tomorrow
and it makes you want to keep everything

but he is gone right now
so, put it away until you are ready to throw it away
you will be ready someday.

talk about it
to your family, friends, journal
anything or anyone you can speak your mind to
don't be afraid to talk about the good times
it will help you feel less bitter

and lastly
love yourself
i know it sounds cliché
but it is so damn important
this is what counts the most
do whatever it takes to love you
one day you will be filled
with so much love for yourself
it will have no room to love him anymore
and that is when the hurting stops

the end

when someone walks out of your life
it is not the end of your story
it is the end of their chapter in your story

you are the author
you must continue writing
this next chapter belongs to you
so, make it a good one

Made in the USA
San Bernardino, CA
16 February 2020